ALL ABOUT INSECTS

ALL ABOUT FIREFLIES

by Golriz Golkar

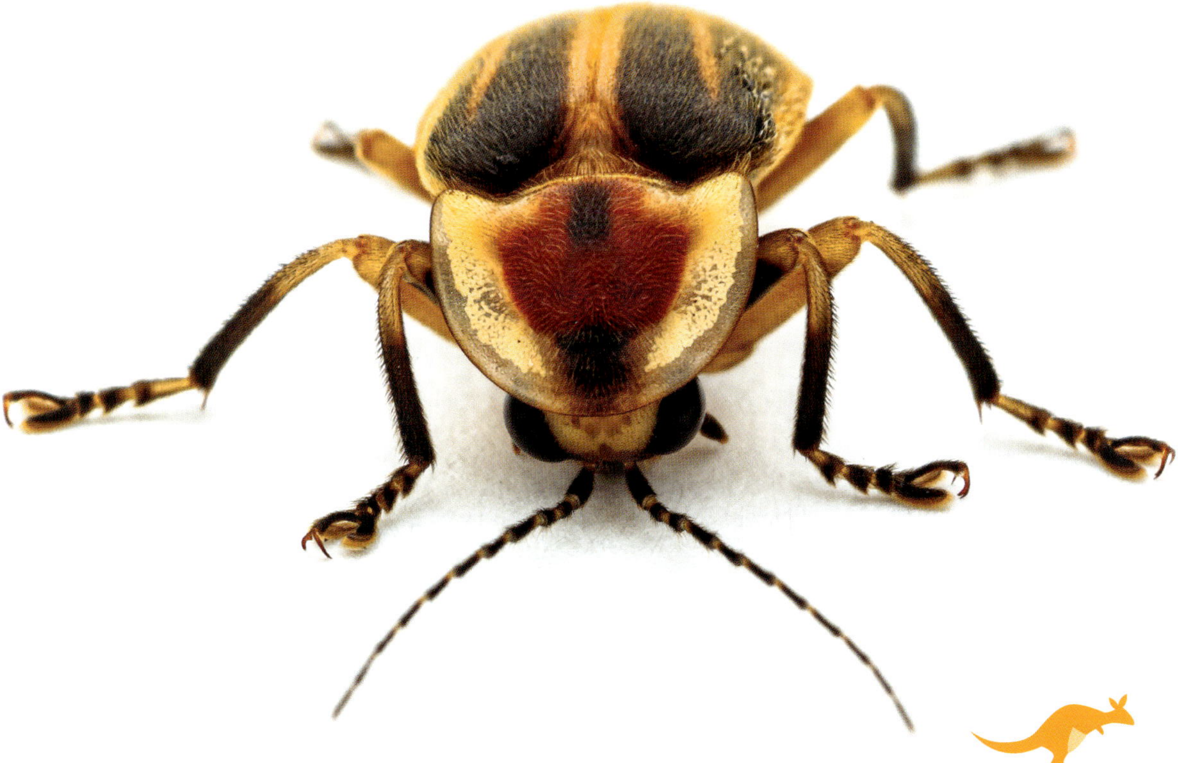

pogo

Ideas for Parents and Teachers

Pogo Books let children practice reading informational text while introducing them to nonfiction features such as headings, labels, sidebars, maps, and diagrams, as well as a table of contents, glossary, and index.

Carefully leveled text with a strong photo match offers early fluent readers the support they need to succeed.

Before Reading

- "Walk" through the book and point out the various nonfiction features. Ask the student what purpose each feature serves.
- Look at the glossary together. Read and discuss the words.

Read the Book

- Have the child read the book independently.
- Invite him or her to list questions that arise from reading.

After Reading

- Discuss the child's questions. Talk about how he or she might find answers to those questions.
- Prompt the child to think more. Ask: Have you ever seen a firefly? What color was its light?

Pogo Books are published by Jump!
5357 Penn Avenue South
Minneapolis, MN 55419
www.jumplibrary.com

Library of Congress Cataloging-in-Publication Data

Names: Golkar, Golriz, author.
Title: All about fireflies / by Golriz Golkar.
Description: Minneapolis, MN: Jump!, Inc., [2025]
Series: All about insects | Includes index.
Audience: Ages 7–10
Identifiers: LCCN 2023050551 (print)
LCCN 2023050552 (ebook)
ISBN 9798889969846 (hardcover)
ISBN 9798889969853 (paperback)
ISBN 9798889969860 (ebook)
Subjects: LCSH: Fireflies—Juvenile literature
Fireflies—Life cycles—Juvenile literature
Classification: LCC QL596.L28 G65 2025 (print)
LCC QL596.L28 (ebook)
DDC 595.76/44—dc23/eng/20231204
LC record available at https://lccn.loc.gov/2023050551
LC ebook record available at https://lccn.loc.gov/2023050552

Editor: Katie Chanez
Designer: Emma Almgren-Bersie

Photo Credits: Suzanne Tucker/Shutterstock, cover; Josiah 'Ant Man' Kilburn/Shutterstock, 1; Piotr Velixar/Shutterstock, 3; Harmonia101/Dreamstime, 4; Ivan Kuzmin/Alamy, 5; blickwinkel/Alamy, 6-7; Aflo Co., Ltd./Alamy, 8-9; Japan's Fireworks/Shutterstock, 9, 19; Henrik Larsson/Shutterstock, 10 (left); WildPictures/Alamy, 10 (right); Stephen Dalton/Minden Pictures/SuperStock, 11; Hyde Peranitti/Shutterstock, 12-13; Unno Kazuo/Minden Pictures, 14-15; Jeff J Daly/Alamy, 16-17; izanbar/iStock, 18; Nicola Villa/Dreamstime, 20-21; khlungcenter/Shutterstock, 21; Chase D'animulls/Shutterstock, 23.

Printed in the United States of America at Corporate Graphics in North Mankato, Minnesota.

TABLE OF CONTENTS

CHAPTER 1

HI, BRIGHT FIREFLY!

A dark **insect** rests on a leaf. It has yellow and orange marks. It has six legs. Two **antennas** feel and smell.

It spreads its wings and takes flight. It lights up! What is this insect? It is a firefly!

Fireflies are **beetles**. There are around 2,000 firefly **species**. Most live in warm, wet areas. Males use wings to fly. Many females do not have wings.

TAKE A LOOK!

What are the parts of a male firefly? Take a look!

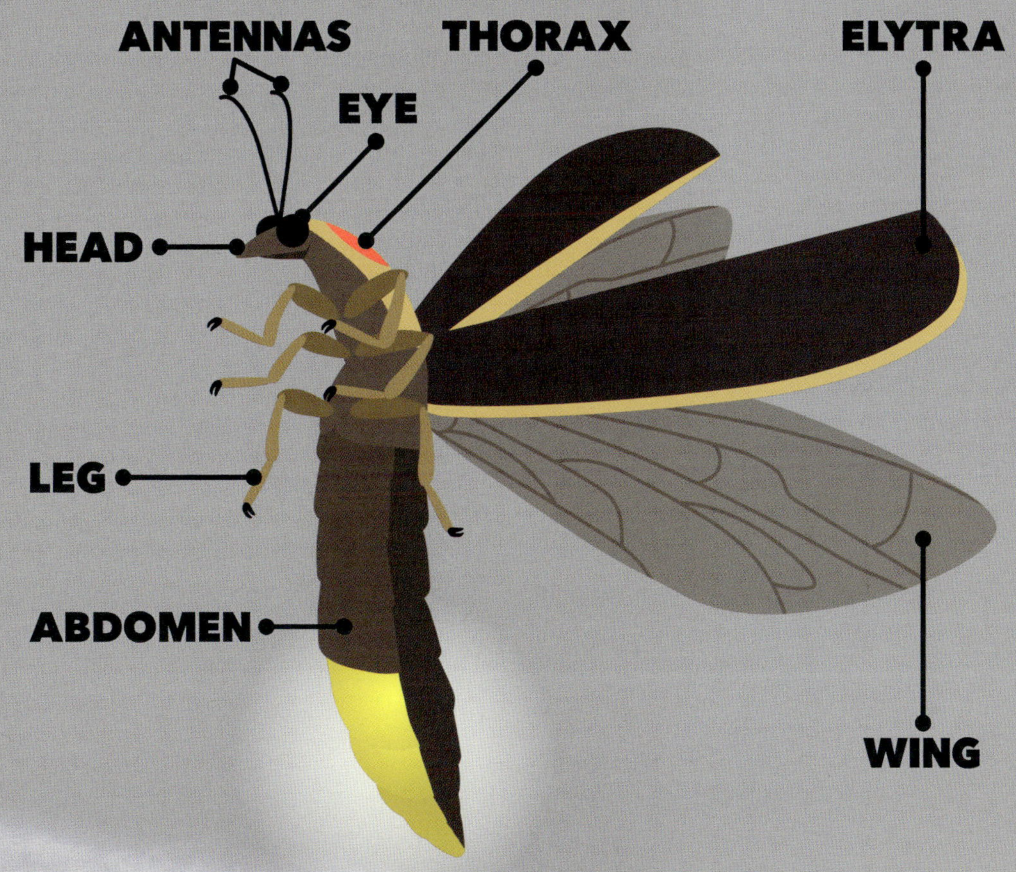

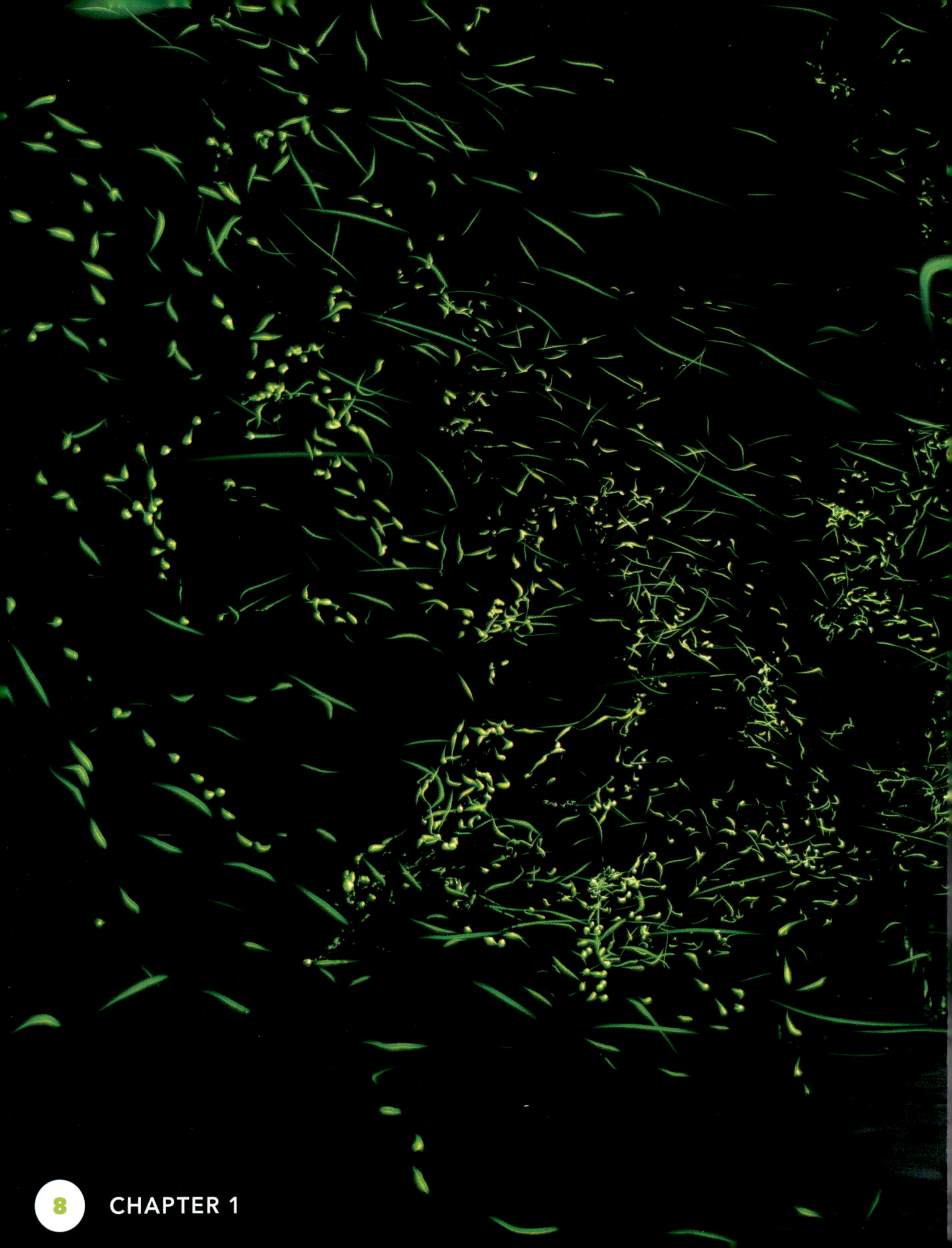

Most fireflies make light. How? They breathe in oxygen. The oxygen enters special **cells**. It mixes with a **chemical**. This makes a flash or glow. Many fireflies make yellow or orange light. Some make blue or green light.

CHAPTER 2

LIFE CYCLE

A firefly's light is a **signal**. It says it is ready to **mate**. When it gets dark, females wait for males to fly by. A male lights up. A female answers with her light. Each species has its own flash or glow pattern.

After mating, female fireflies lay eggs in wet areas. They lay them in the ground or under leaves. The eggs glow. The light scares **predators** away. The eggs have **poison** in them. Animals that eat them can get sick.

After two to four weeks, **larvae** hatch from the eggs. They live in wet soil. They eat slugs, worms, snails, and caterpillars. Some catch **prey** by squirting poison in them. The prey cannot move. The larvae eat them!

DID YOU KNOW?

Before laying eggs, some female fireflies eat males. Why? The male's poison goes into the female's eggs. This keeps the eggs extra safe from predators.

snail
larva

Fireflies can stay in the larvae stage for up to two years. In spring, they change into **pupae**. Some pupae are underground. Others stick to trees. They grow and become adults.

TAKE A LOOK!

Fireflies grow in four stages. Take a look!

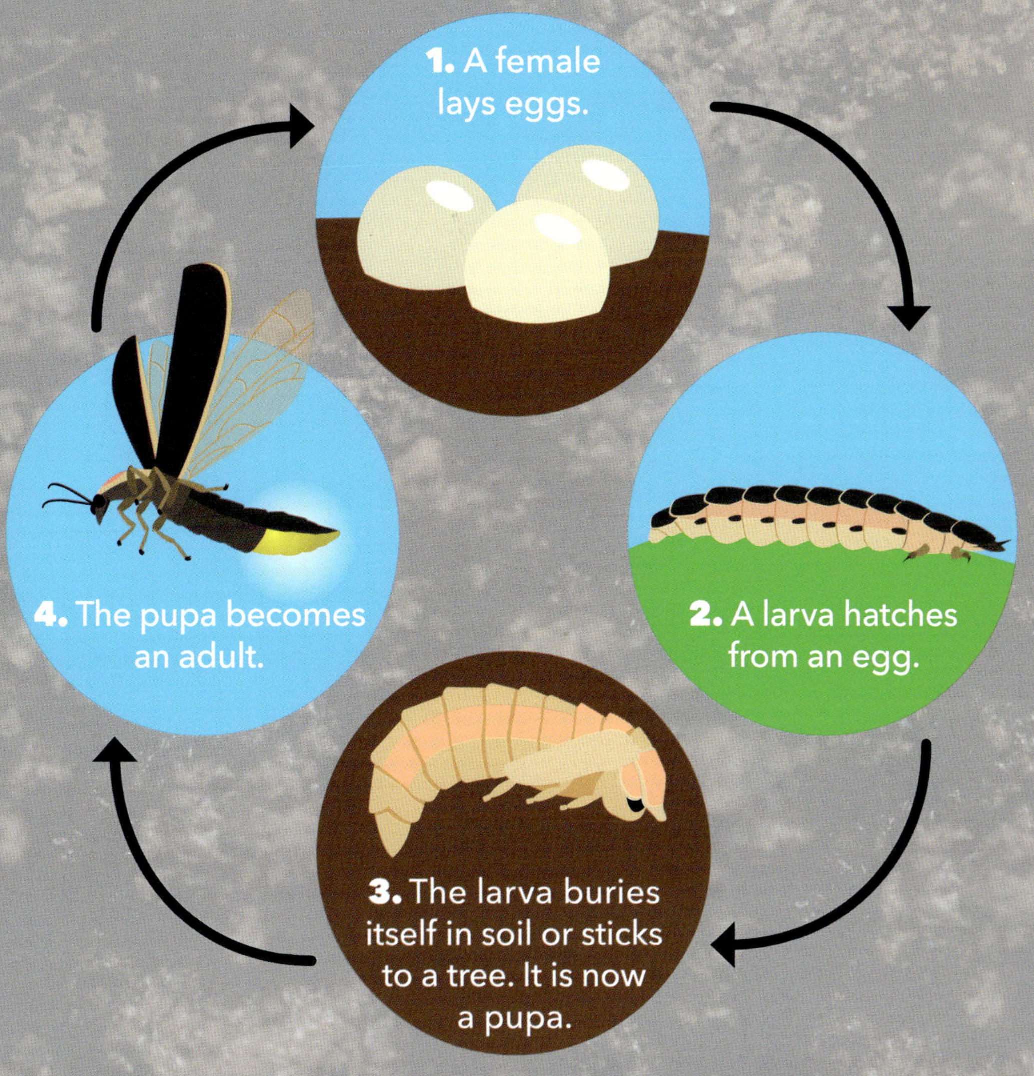

Adults live up to two months. Many do not eat. They spend their time mating and laying eggs.

DID YOU KNOW?

Some firefly species do not make light. They use smells to find mates. Males give off smells. Females answer with their own smells.

CHAPTER 3

TWINKLE TIME

Few animals eat fireflies. Most are afraid of the light. But frogs, birds, and spiders sometimes eat them. Frogs may light up if they eat too many!

Most fireflies are **nocturnal**. They rest on leaves during the day. They fly at night.

Fireflies are easiest to find on warm summer nights. Have you ever seen a twinkling firefly?

DID YOU KNOW?

Some firefly species flash together in groups. Some flash at the same time. Others flash seconds apart. This makes waves of light!

ACTIVITIES & TOOLS

TRY THIS!

TWINKLING FIREFLY

Make a twinkling firefly in this fun activity!

What You Need:

- 1 plastic egg that opens in the middle
- black permanent marker
- 2 black pipe cleaners
- scissors
- glue
- duct tape
- battery-operated tealight

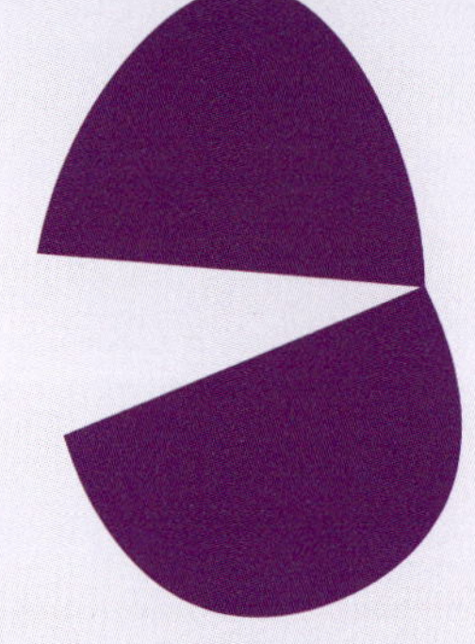

1. Draw two large eyes and a smile on the rounded bottom half of the plastic egg.
2. Cut both pipe cleaners in half. Cross three pieces to make a star shape. Twist the middle so the pipe cleaners hold together. Bend the ends to make legs. Turn the egg horizontally to make the body. Glue the legs to the underside of the egg. Do not glue the egg's opening.
3. Bend the last piece of pipe cleaner into a V to make antennas. Glue the point above the face.
4. Cut a two-inch (5-cm) piece of duct tape. Fold it in half.
5. Cut the folded duct tape to make two wings. Tape the wings to the top of the pointed half of the egg.
6. Turn on the tealight. Place it inside the egg. Snap the egg shut. Now you have a firefly!

GLOSSARY

antennas: Feelers on the head of an insect.

beetles: The most common type of insect. Beetles are insects whose wings are covered by elytra.

cells: The smallest units of an animal or plant.

chemical: A liquid the body produces.

insect: A small animal with three pairs of legs, one or two pairs of wings, and three main body parts.

larvae: Insects in the stage of growth between eggs and pupae.

mate: To come together to produce babies.

nocturnal: Active at night.

poison: A substance that can harm or kill a person, animal, or plant.

predators: Animals that hunt other animals for food.

prey: Animals that are hunted by other animals for food.

pupae: Insects in the stage of growth between larvae and adults.

signal: A sign that sends a message or warning.

species: One of the groups into which similar animals and plants are divided.

INDEX

TO LEARN MORE

Finding more information is as easy as 1, 2, 3.

1. Go to www.factsurfer.com
2. Enter "fireflies" into the search box.
3. Choose your book to see a list of websites.